Still

DIANA

A POETS PERSPECTIVE

VERONICA CARTER

www.TrueVinePublishing.org

Still Diana
Veronica Carter

Published by
True Vine Publishing Co.
810 Dominican Dr.
Nashville, TN 37228

ISBN: 978-1-962783-09-5 Paperback
ISBN: 978-1-962783-06-4 eBook

Printed In the United States of America—First Printing

Dedication

I want to dedicate this book to my wonderful family, whom I love and cherish dearly.

To my amazing daughter, Destiny, who constantly challenges me and reminds me that life is not just about me. To my son, Isaiah, who has always been my hero. He once said, "Mom, you shall live and not die and declare the works of the Lord," as some scriptures describe the wonderful and marvelous works of the Lord. My oldest daughter, Mieya, carries a unique weight of unconditional love that spreads wherever she goes. And, of course, my husband Ronnie, my partner of 22 years, who continues to lead our family with strength and love, always covering us in prayer.

I also want to express gratitude to Pastor Charles Gibson of Breakthrough Church, Dr. Timothy Sloan of The Luke Church in Houston,

Texas, and Rabbi Schneider of Discovering the Jewish Jesus. I also want to mention inspiring figures like Bishop Dale C. Bronner and Pastor John Bevere, each contributing to the knowledge of being driven by eternity.

To the God of Abraham and Israel, your grace is boundless, and your glory knows no limits. Serving is our unique representation within the house and beyond for the purpose of the Kingdom of God.

In closing, I want to share a message with young people, all people, and God's people: lay up treasures in heaven! As Matthew 6:19 advises, do not accumulate treasures on earth where they can be destroyed or stolen. Instead, focus on storing up treasures in heaven, where they are safe from decay and theft (Matthew 6:20).

Still Diana

Amidst the cheering crowds and distant speculation, a scene unfolds with profound beauty and grace. What would Diana, observing the four white horses led by two, carrying the Prince and Princess into marital bliss, say? To Prince William and Prince Harry, I commend your best efforts. Your armor of valor and shoulders of preparation set a high standard, making it challenging for anyone to step into your shoes. As a mere onlooker, I can't fathom the weight you carry.

Certainly, royalty brings perks, entitlements, and prestige, but what if there's no harbor to anchor it all? Sons of an angel, my brothers, the task may be too monumental for you alone to heal our land. Perhaps, consider joining us in prayer, thinking about the divine portal that Heaven invariably offers on the horizon.

Life, incredibly precious, prompts a question: why do we wait so long to appreciate someone with flowers, like roses in a field? Life itself can be extraordinary, akin to the silent warriors of yester-years whose messages of hope continue to inspire us today.

Let's not forget the teachings of Billy Graham, the wisdom of Dr. Myles Monroe, the compassion of Billy Joe Daugherty, and the straightforward teachings of Pastor Charles Stanley. These immortal giants, along with Pastor Charles Gibson, Sandra Kennedy, Tony Evans, Rabbi Schneider, Dr. Timothy W. Sloan, Pastors Sedell and Yolanda Campbell, endure and fight alongside us today. They echo the comforting words of Jeremiah 29:11: "For I know the thoughts that I think toward you, says the Lord, thoughts of peace and not of evil, to give you a future and a hope."

None of us truly comprehend the immense grace required for individuals, including pastors, to navigate the challenges of perseverance and commitment. Can you imagine being a pastor in today's complex society? Let's be honest; it's no small feat.

Oh Lord, the anticipation is great, and the sky unfolds, captivating the heavens. The rocks glisten, sparkle, and shine, and raindrops illuminate the person below, reflecting the divine. However, the conversation among subjects and civilians has grown toxic, manipulated, and overemphasized. It's driving brother against brother, tearing apart families, pitting cities against countries, and ultimately turning people against one another. Have we forgotten that we are all in this together?

City shelters are overcrowded, and juvenile detention centers are repurposed as housing facilities to address the expanding needs of an aging-out foster care system. Homelessness is becoming a widespread documentary playing out before our eyes. People from all walks of life are being forced out of their homes, often through no fault of their own, and many are just one economic disaster away from calamity.

Let's open our eyes at town hall and look around. The documentary of homelessness is spreading like an open playbook. People, including those considered elites, are being evacuated. The strain is felt by all, and I proudly say there's nothing wrong with trading in cans and bottles. We must acknowledge our shared experience and work together to address these pressing issues.

For countless individuals, prayer becomes a solace as we express gratitude for the basics: clothes on our backs, shoes on our feet, and a roof over our heads. In the midst of the frenetic pulse of today's society, survival has become a shared journey, traversed by both the affluent and the impoverished, creating a stored-up middle-class alliance.

For those of us bearing the responsibility of caring for the wounded and those unable to care for themselves, it's essential to take a step back and assess our own well-being. This is a dry place where suffering is endured in silence. Acknowledge that your situation is significant and may be too much for one person to handle alone.

With bills accumulating and funds dwindling, the question of being a giver arises. The truth is, like many of you, I am a continual work in progress. Attempting to reset and align my priorities with God's, I find myself physically and mentally drained, contemplating throwing in the towel. I've exhausted every natural means, and the thought of seeking help from others has its challenges.

It's often said that God won't give us more than we can bear, but my back is heavy, my shoulders strained, and I feel cornered. The way forward seems unclear, and the burden feels overwhelming.

Yet, like my sister Diana, I hold onto hope because the dream I carry is not about me. It's an eternal weight of glory that must be fulfilled for the chapter to be complete. In this dry desert place, I activate my activity, walking towards the goals I've set for my life, holding onto the dream with great expectancy. Yes, my problem is big, but my God is bigger. With good cheer and constant praise, I envision myself daily fulfilling the promises He gave.

As we delve deeper into this critical hour of being fit for the Kingdom, uncharted territory for some, I admit I am also at an absolute loss. However, one thing remains certain, Isaiah 55:9 declares, "For as the heavens are higher than the earth, So are My ways higher than your ways, And My thoughts than your thoughts." In a world already crazy, how do we navigate and protect the innocent and the truly young at heart?

Taking a step back and reflecting on the pulse of the youth, I ask about your family's portrait of justification. When you've gone as far as you can for those you adore, remember the grace once extended to you. Recall the humility of the heart and the prayer for infinite longing. My ultimate desire is to be kept, as expressed in Psalm 42:1, "As the hart panteth after the water brooks, so panteth my soul after thee, O God. Help us, Lord! Help me!"

Navigating the thin line between love and hate, be cautious in condemning others. Consider if you'd rather be a stain of representation in Congress where our country flourishes or contribute to a paralyzed nation. Are you prepared to humble yourself and love again? What energy level are you turning up or dialing down for yourself? These are questions to ponder in our collective journey.

The enemy strategically preys on our strengths to fuel pride and exploits our weaknesses to lead us into sin. In this tireless pursuit and the sting of love for the unimpressed, it's essential to extend leniency to both past and present, acknowledging the labor involved.

Expressing gratitude for a calm spirit and a relaxed state of being, I can sit quietly, not just in my own space, but purposefully in the space of others without prejudgment. It's a moment to ask for divine intervention for myself and recognize the interconnectedness of all as my brothers and sisters. Giving ourselves a little grace is crucial in this hour of great awareness. Consider desensitizing from the world one day a week to healthily replenish.

In this discipline of Breakthrough Church, Psalm 68:33 is a plea to God, who rides across the highest heavens and thunders with a mighty voice. As we traverse the cobblestone streets of London, Rome, Italy, and the downtown abbeys of America, conflicting energy resonates worldwide. The sound wave is not just a minor element but an overlapping indictment of the mind, questioning not just getting to worthy but the worthiness of the fight, for all of us.

The cobwebs of yesterday sting like the mechanical swaps of today. Instead of wondering what Princess Diana would say, the focus shifts to What Would God Say! With the same energy and intent, let's reflect on Psalm 68:33, inviting divine intervention. Remembering the invasive polarized paparazzi and any two no-name individuals of a supposed private institute, let's not go there. Let's not forget; let's not pretend to imagine.

My God, the same today, yesterday, tomorrow, and forevermore. As the state of the world descends towards the ugliest levels of defaults,

Veronica Carter

where does that leave us in this hour of distress, legal and otherwise? Refusing to delve into the politics of prayer, I express my gratitude for prayer, an indispensable element for my survival. In this critical hour, some things cannot be taught; they have to be observed.

No worries; I am grateful and appreciative for the House of Prayer, your authentic expression and version of thought articulated. Have you ever sat under the melting, saturated, thunderous aroma of prayer, experiencing the blizzard rainfall and smokey white streamline? There is a heavenly mist coming from the House of God, a kind of residue that engages, embarks, interlocks, and overlaps, sending forth its own radio atmospheric frequency of highlighted rays, perpetually affirming, "I am absolutely approved, sealed, stamped, and highly favored by God!" (John 10:27)

Key to this is recognizing the voice of God.

Lord, help me to be a good listener in this hour, not jumping ahead in any area or situation. Thankful for godly reconnections and divine hookups, I acknowledge how God sends laborers across our paths to remind us it's not about us. When family or loved ones pray for you, those prayers can be tangibly felt. Consider that in your secret boiler room, the steamed locomotive produces praise, exudes worship, and releases smoke from your reaffirming pressing place, penetrating the heart of God gladly from your bended knees.

Prayer is the powerhouse locomotive, and its exhaust travels aboard, bursting through the world's largest chimneys, dispersing sparks that rain down God's justice for you and me.

In addition, there is a supernatural banner highlighted by the grace of God, upon which a mother or grandmother knows and can relate to the soundtrack of prayer in a way similar to recognizing the smell and fragrance of her own off-spring. It's an indescribable and beautiful connection, akin to the innate instinct of love and nurturing care found even in animals. When we cry out "Abba, Father" in prayer, we know that God is for us.

In this critical hour, if anyone could take center stage, it would be that of a loving grandmother. Regardless of the dynamics or the mathematics of the relationship, a loving grandmother will always find a way to express love, crossing ponds, lakes, rivers, and seas to cherish you and yours. So, the question that strikes the air is not which beloved son Princess Diana would visit first. If we were to wonder or speculate, perhaps, after traveling abroad and living her best life, enjoying highlighted blossoms, inherited royal grace, and enchanting sceneries, she might, as a mother, choose to be with the son closest to her at the time.

Without a doubt, the dream could include the rapture of a loving, never-ending embrace, the warmth of a tender kiss, and the rush of unconditional love. It's a love that is intertwined and wrapped all in one - the kind of love that brings anticipation and cannot hardly wait. Regardless of the location, a mother's reinforcement is love, and the expansion of that is the glorious laughter of the bubbling bounce on the knee. Not to mention the joy of those little hands posing, stretching, and reaching up towards everyone together so graciously.

God is my plus one, without question and without compromise! I've got a whopping yawl! Let me reiterate: I've got a whopping yawl! Under the penalty and punishment of Jesus Christ, what I thought was a grand idea - one of those ideas with a servant's perspective in ministry parallel to the interaction and agenda of TikTok. Everything must be done in decency and in order.

Am I right about it! Sharing ideas with others is one thing, but when your idea involves ministry, it would indeed be wise to direct it under the guidance of leadership. This ensures that the idea aligns with the boundaries and limits of interactions set by the ministry. Now, let me try to explain since we often think we know it all.

On a Tuesday morning, in the first week of the first month, at 6:00 am, there was a prayer service orchestrated by Pastor and First Lady Michelle Gibson, highlighting the growth of the ministry. Understanding the Council Chambers of God's grace, it seemed clear.

However, when attempting to attend the prayer service that morning, there was a metaphorical "Madea-type whopping" in the natural. It felt like the stern yet loving correction you might get from someone saying, "Didn't I tell you so?" It was as if a belt was tagging, swinging, and spanking to emphasize the point.

On Wednesday, still very apologetic and attempting to attend the prayer service, the metaphorical belt came from up in the air, ready to come down full throttle. Understanding the sacredness of God's house, I recognized that unlike the four walls of any structure or organization, God's house is sacred.

Not easily offended, I remained under the Council Chambers of God's grace, recognizing the purpose of legacy that remains supreme. As a mother introducing a servant's heart, I reflect on Fit for the Kingdom and those committed soldiers and warriors who, some no longer here, others still standing valiantly within the gap for us.

In this moment of chastisement, I am reminded of who He is - the Lord God Almighty. With humility of heart and humbleness of spirit, even if I were one of many, I couldn't give flowers in a field or roses in a vineyard. What I can do in this moment of chastisement for Fit for the Kingdom is share my experience unashamedly and wholeheartedly. I boldly confess that my mind is clear, my spirit is free, and I will seek first the Kingdom of God and His righteousness, knowing that all will be added to me.

Are you already grateful for growth, success, and progress? Sometimes, worry and uncertainty creep in—feeling the pressure, noticing the rising tension. Picture this: the tea is brewing, blueberries are in the blender, and your phone is ringing for that important meeting next week. It's easy to overthink and worry about being on time.

In today's world, our children often dream bigger dreams for us than we do for ourselves. Some are determined to achieve those dreams at any cost, even if it means stepping out of their comfort zones. You might say this isn't a new phenomenon, but it's essential to consider the toll it takes on their character—faith, leadership, and potential.

Parents, now is the time for a meaningful conversation with our young ones. The cycle of deception is in full swing, and the temptation to engage in questionable activities is pervasive. It's crucial to realize that they may be going through challenges, too. Yet, we often find ourselves blaming them for actions we might have taken in the past, only with more secrecy and manipulation.

Let's pause and reflect on the situation. It's time for an open dialogue with our youth, acknowledging their struggles while guiding them towards a path of integrity and genuine success.

Favoring the exclusive Royal Elites, absent from the negotiations – merely a suggestion, not representation, certainly not for action or reality, not this time. Speaking hypothetically, as a 20-year advisor to Servitude and a 10-year member

Veronica Carter

of the Vice Squad of patriotisms, does that auto-
matically make you, me, or anyone else a gate-
keeper of service? Can one claim a monopoly on
servitude after just a few weeks?

It's intriguing, and your service is acknowl-
edged, time is valued. However, let's be cautious
not to elevate ourselves too high. Your extended
tenure doesn't grant a monopoly on any form of
servitude. It's essential to recognize that. Your
halt, suited and booted, may unintentionally
transform into an idol—a mere act of perform-
ance, reminiscent of Eastern cinema, meticu-
lously crafted under watchful eyes.

How do we, and can we, discuss respect with
others when we ourselves carry traces of entitle-
ment that warrant podcast covers and interviews?
It's a delicate balance worth considering.

Is there anyone ready to join me in celebrat-
ing Him to the point where I'm moved to blush at
the mention of His name—Jesus! And not be-

cause of the "shoulda, coulda, wouldas" my mom warned me about. She tried to stop me, as did my dad, uncle, big brother, and mentor. They all invested time to teach me.

To some of the young people out there, you're making it challenging to communicate. I express gratitude for divine intervention, always guiding me to carry on and have real conversations. For those who believe they know everything, time is running short for all of us. Let's embrace humility and openness to learn from each other.

Still think you're too old to get a whopping? Well, guess what? Just yesterday, I got a good old-fashioned slap. It wasn't just a tap—it was one of those wake-up calls. "Hush now! Get yourself together!" he said. Whether it was backhanded or delivered straight on, my head is still spinning. But here I am, standing tall, shoulders somewhat firm.

Veronica Carter

That mental torment, that igloo of distress in my mind? It's not even a fleeting thought, not an inkling, or an ism. I've shaken it off and moved forward.

Realizing that I come from something greater, I must be a part of something much, much bigger. In this understanding, we will always rise in triumph. The sound of release is so powerful that it's no longer troubling. I'm still standing within the same day, scratching and rubbing my head, wondering what it was, what I thought it was. Life can be like a jungle sometimes, Lord God. My mind often wanders.

From servitude to sonship, in the absence of humor, all we can do is laugh. 1 Thessalonians 5:16-18 in the Bible talks about rejoicing always, praying without ceasing, and giving thanks in everything, for this is the will of God in Christ Jesus for you. Also, Romans 14:16-18 advises not letting what is good be spoken of as evil. The

Kingdom of God is not just about eating and drinking but about righteousness, peace, and joy in the Holy Spirit. Anyone who serves Christ in this way pleases God and receives human approval. That's His word, ladies and gentlemen.

Now, let's fortify the remaining branches, for He is the Potter, and we are the clay. We live and grow side by side, each of us struggling to take root and reach for a bit of sunlight in the morning rush. It's not always about outdoing one another, though sometimes it is, and that's just a part of who we are, to be honest.

We all have a limited time to express ourselves. Most of us want to leave a lasting, memorable impression. Some aspire to stand tall, spread our wings, and blossom in the sunlight, truly understanding what it means to live freely and calmly. Despite the challenges, and even in the harshest climates, the environment you create is dictated by the soil you choose.

Oh, but God! In the end, negativity will be weeded out and overturned. So, my brothers and sisters, sprout anyway, grow together relentlessly, generation after generation. Let the grasslands be inclusive and always well-preserved.

The young and old are together at last, and many of us are still screaming inside, yearning to break free from the internal turmoil. Are there any encouraging responses among us, beyond the usual advice to pull up your pants or give your seat to an elderly person? Respecting our elders, saying "Yes, Ma'am" or "No, Sir" – these are signs of respect, young people. It goes a long way.

I understand the need for accountability – checking if the countertop is clean, the trash is taken out without being reminded. Emotions silenced for real this time, but with much respect toward each of us. God is above your entire mountain.

Still Diana

The most captivating trial of the day is the sound in the atmosphere that lands on the surface. Tyre Nichols' talent is explosive, granting each of us the right to exist. Your unique manhood is just beginning, Tyre Nichols, an amateur photographer whose skills shine among us, taking flight and captivating our hearts. You unite the best of us, reminiscent only to the sky above, a thread that challenges and connects us. God, continue to shine with and for us!

God with us! Gone too soon! Manuel Esteban Paez, your meditation in pause and gesture for life pronounced it in such a remarkable way. It's remarkable to most, unknown to some, liberating us all and bringing each of us a little closer than ever before. Your journey and pursuit of peaceful protest define who we are and who we all aspire to be at our core.

Have we forgotten the summer of 2020? As alarming as this may be, people tend to forget how we all came together as one unit, one body on equal grounds, standing tall, unhinged, unafraid to the point of risking our very own lives in the midst of disease and death. Still, we did that, ladies and gentlemen—all of us together! Because we all have the right to exist.

In a world with trigger-happy assailants and licensed gun-toting disturbed systemic individuals, protest remains our God-given quintessential American constitutional fundamental right, especially in this hour like never before. With erupting greenhouse gas emissions, melting polar ice caps, rising temperatures globally, disastrous floods, broken levees, toxic smoke, underlying dangerous chemicals overshadowing the sky and polluting the environment and atmosphere—not just in one place but too many places to count.

Climate change is not just a worldwide emergency; it's a priority that is breathing health, healing, and restoration. Are we listening?

Someone call 911; I hear you, Holy Spirit shout out to First Lady Michelle Gibson! In fact, shout out to all First Ladies around the globe and throughout this nation standing firm in this critical hour, valiantly within the gap for us all today. And shout out to you, Pastor Charles Gibson; I hear you, I see you. That is purpose! I am the head and not the tail, I am above and not beneath. I am a lender, and not a borrower. That part! And the lesson of Aaron's oily beard is a lesson of unity. Psalm 133:2 illustrates, "Behold, how good and how pleasant it is for brothers to dwell together in unity! It is like the precious oil upon the head, coming down upon the beard, even Aaron's beard, coming down from the edge of his robes.

Psalm 91:1 says, "Whoever dwells in the shelter of the Most High will rest in the shadow of the Almighty." There's a scripture in the Bible, Matthew 10:14, that advises, "If anyone does not welcome you or listen to your words, leave that home or town and shake the dust off your feet."

When we unintentionally find ourselves on the wrong street or enter the wrong driveway, as we all do, tragic events unfold. Today, we hear of unthinkable incidents where innocent individuals, like an honor student returning home from school to pick up his siblings, face unexpected violence. Knocking on a stranger's door turns into a tragedy, with this young student being shot twice for a simple act.

Lord, help us! Help me! While recovery is needed, the bitterness of the situation is overwhelming. But God, this time. It's a time to pause the rebellious spirit and turn up, always, yeah! Turn it up for Jesus!

Now that the knights have lowered their swords, and your defenses are on guard for piercing criticism, who is it that you condemn? Do we not understand that God's love for His people transcends personal feelings? Your church hurt doesn't outweigh mine, and letting it drag you down the road of superiority is a mirror worth pondering. Help us, Lord! Help me!

I want to emphasize that I do not have the authority to determine heaven or hell for you or anyone else, and neither do you. If you find yourself shell-shocked, stuck in a lane of half-twisted conspiracy theories, detached from reasoning, conversation, or even a breath of normalcy, it raises the question: is this the internet, AI, or just you?

Some individuals are left excessively alone behind closed doors, stewing in their own special sauce. Have you noticed how these people sometimes resemble the negative consumption they've accumulated, not necessarily formed but wounded and scared, resembling the walking dead? What are they in danger of, you might wonder? Thinking, "I have to get him before he

Veronica Carter

gets me." Damn!

Really, y'all! At least let me come up for some air in this fight. The only thing I have left is my love, and you want to take that away. Hold on, love is like my toothpaste; come on now, don't take my toothpaste! Just like that? Not this time, you've gone too far. People, that's all I've got—my love. And if I'm ever going to come out swinging in any fight, especially in this one, I lay it down, people. Not quietly or restrained because it is the God of Abraham, Isaac, and Jacob who handles me! Yes, Lord, thank you for helping us! Thank you in advance for helping me! Because in this hour, I have no choice but to humbly lay it down; it was never my fight to begin with. It's way too big for me!

If we could allow God Almighty to swoop in like Captain Sava Gee, known to us all, or as an imaginary friend; an enlightened cartoon character with Marvel-like enhanced characteristics from the Throne Room of Grace, representing Happy hey Happy! In assistance with DC Young Fly! Chin up! Chest out! "I'm still here!" And if we could perhaps use you as well in this critical hour, yes, you, my brother, and my sister, as the one that God has chosen; you, a uniquely qualified superhero. Humbly putting on the Whole Armor of God—look it up in Ephesians 6, which talks about standing firm with the belt of truth buckled around your waist, the breastplate of righteousness in place, and your feet fitted with the readiness that comes from the gospel of peace.

In addition to all this, take up the Shield of Faith, with which you can extinguish all the flaming arrows of the evil one. Take the Helmet of Salvation and the Sword of the Spirit, which is the Word of God. Finally, be strong in the Lord and in His mighty power. If you could, go there, really; deep dive with us—DC Young Fly, you, and me! We all have our very own superheroes in character and mind today, right! May I proceed if we could swim, perhaps underneath a shallow bridge of anchored ships, both small and gigantic? Those ships that are sometimes reluctant to go out to sea, and those arriving early, coming into the port to dock.

Still, Superhero, if you would leap, climb, dance a dynamic beat. With your arms and hands wet, and rubbery extended, swinging from pillar to pillar, launching forward, with your feet hitting snowboarding; onto grazed grasslands above high level, steep hill sights and sliding up and down. Then, your feet, now magnetically clutching, launch, producing its own longboard attached from a position of pause, then ignited by the flame of the Throne Room of Grace upon the highest of mountain peaks. Directly bursting through the clouds, morning blaze of 9:00 am Bible Study. "Speak, Lord, speak to me! Praise break! Sing your song, Earth Angels!" He might just say to you, Practical Son or Daughter, just as DC Young Fly has continued to do.

Again, are we listening? As He slows down with his right foot, surfboarding with his left foot, jumping again, and launching forward with his right foot longboarding, cruising, rolling, and pressing ever so gently. Skkirtt! And in your face, coming to a complete hard stop! God is asking you! In fact, He is asking all of us in this critical hour.

Why not you, my child, and where have you been? Transition from that of the varsity elites, the screaming shouts echoing across different lanes, the breeze of the arena, and the soccer field, all set up for that particular championship game. Whether won by a single kick of the field goal or a major touchdown, or perhaps the win of a three-pointer shot from your favorite basketball team. Life is a win for all of us, simply to exist in a world gone too far. That's right, we still win at and in between all levels of life. To live life out loud is a celebration all its own, especially in a world of madness. Life is awe, wow, absolutely extraordinary, great, unlimited. To draw from that gigantic crowd of joy, shouts, and the praise of the hurrah of that glorious crown of our own made-up cheerleading squad, perfumed by droplets of radiance, called out, shouted, in tune, then repeated by your very own sensitive blow tube, multiplied times the loudest praise of worship, valiantly recorded and victoriously vindicated because, once again, it is the God of Abraham, Isaac, and Jacob who restores and redeems me and you, always.

Now, on my way to victory and moving on up like the Jeffersons, I would share with Prince William and Prince Harry how their mother, Princess Diana, remains a friend in my head wholeheartedly. In closing, I am wise enough to realize that only a selected few of us have what we call true friendships. I am wise enough to know that, however, if I were privileged enough to have a friend like Princess Diana, and if I could perhaps sit across the table with her at our local Starbucks simply to share the latest tea on the menu, I believe our conversation would go like any other supporting mother, grandmother, sister girl, friend.

As I approach my flight back to the mainland, floating across the reservoirs of Rome, Italy, and Paris with my own two sons, perhaps leaning on one shoulder while outwardly and on purpose extending my hand to my other son. First of all, grateful to still be here and clothed in my right mind, privileged in part as an unstudied subservient driven towards God's divine apprenticeship of eternity. Now, Veronica, leaning towards the robust attributes of Rome, enchanted and intrigued by its amazing artists, and of course, its unbelievable magnificent exquisite one-of-a-kind architecture. No wonder it has some of the world's greatest lovers of our history.

I want to tell you that love is important for the world. I truly believe in my heart that the world would be a better place if we all shared enduring love. It's the little things that matter, like when I saw Cardi B's husband, Offset, walk the red carpet with their kids at the premiere of the Little Mermaid, starring Halle Bailey. It was such an amazing and beautiful event. Shoutout to Offset and Cardi B for making it special for all of us!

I don't have any strong connections to symbols or traditions related to the monarchy. I don't wish harm on anyone, whether they are involved with the monarchy or not. I just want to show respect to those whom Princess Diana loved. I remember Princess Diana bringing people from different cultures together around the world through her stance on political issues like land-mines and other tragedies of war.

I truly believe that Princess Diana loved all of us. You know how people sometimes say someone "loves hard"? Well, I think she embod-ied a selfless kind of love – the type that doesn't expect anything in return. It's that rare kind of love where just having the person's presence is more than enough. It's quite a profound and somewhat intimidating idea. Imagine if that kind of love could be more prevalent today; it's chal-lenging to fathom, especially in our world.

Unfortunately, there's a tendency to believe in falsehoods rather than the truth. Too much time has been wasted, and there's been silence for far too long. All I have is my faith in the Lord and Savior, Jesus. The supernatural release of God doesn't need interruption; it operates in its own time, fast and furious, with a unique justifi-cation. I've come to realize that the illusion is no more, but it took a bold, global attempt to take that love away from me – a love that was always shown as if I'm just not good enough. It's disheartening.

It seems like you'd rather give me the leftovers of yourself instead of offering the best. That's pretty harsh, but I'll speak the truth. In this moment, it feels like you all are quite coldhearted. Regardless, you go ahead with that, because I'm going to keep it real. When people reveal their true selves, it's crucial to believe them.

No need to worry, though. I find solace in Revelation 22:7 – "Look, I am coming soon! Blessed is the one who keeps the words of the prophecy written in this scroll." It's always your choice which parts to edit or discard.

We rely on the King of Kings and the Lord God Almighty to keep us afloat every day. As Psalm 126:2 says, "The joy of the Lord is my strength." Laughter is a beautiful gift, a burst of joy from deep within. It's that uncontrollable laughter that bubbles up, and no matter how hard you try to stifle it, it just keeps coming, bringing a refreshing and unquenchable joy.

Oh, taste and see that the Lord God Almighty is good, considering the kind and benevolent nature of God. He alone desires the best for you, awakening an appetite within. I find it intriguing, like when given the task to read Philippians Chapters 1-4 for seven days straight, noticing how it emphasizes over 16 times to "Rejoice" and speaks of "Great Joy." Read it for yourself and consider the beauty of that message. Now, let's divert from our selfish ambitions and controlling tendencies.

As the legendary Winans Brothers and Sisters would ask, the questions linger: Will I ever leave you? Will I do your will? And when will Jesus return? The answer is a resounding no, for my God will never leave me. I will always strive to say yes to your will, and the return of Jesus is imminent (John 3:16).

Reflecting on Deuteronomy 5:16, which commands us to honor our father and mother, promising long days and prosperity in the land. This upcoming holiday season, let's keep that in mind. Imagine a heavenly conversation, the warmth and beat of legendary figures like Princess Diana, the late Michael Jackson, Whitney Houston, Mr. Rogers, and the marvelous Bob Ross. Each artist in their own right, I can't help but wonder what their conversation would be like if they were with us today. AI people, pay attention! Imagine the dialogue among these selfless servants in our time.

Certainly, let's continue with 2 Timothy 3. The passage goes on to describe how in the last days, perilous times will come. Men will exhibit characteristics such as being lovers of them-selves, lovers of money, boastful, proud, blasphemers, disobedient to parents, unthankful, and unholy. As you pointed out, it also mentions being unloving. It's a poignant reflection on the challenging qualities that may manifest in people during these times. Feel free to elaborate or share your thoughts on this specific aspect of the scripture.

It's true that some of us are adept at concealing the superficial aspects of a poisonous and tormenting spirit within ourselves. This hidden struggle may persist, seeking not only to attach itself to us but also waiting for the opportune moment to lead us back to destructive old habits.

In these moments, we turn to you, Lord Jesus, asking for your grace and unconditional love to pull on our heartstrings. Help us to speak highly of those who are no longer with us, even those who may have wronged or enslaved us. Guard us against the enemy of comparisons, so we don't get distracted by false perceptions or

Veronica Carter

actions.

Ephesians 6:4 advises fathers not to provoke
their children to wrath but to bring them up in
the training and admonition of the Lord. Share
with them the hidden wisdom and counsel found
in passages like Psalm 116, 117, and 118, em-
phasizing the importance of paying attention to
the threes in the Bible. These passages reveal
God's strategies and counsel that come from
reading and meditating on His word.

James 1:16-17 cautions us not to be de-
ceived, emphasizing that every good and perfect
gift comes from above. In simpler terms, there is
nothing good for us outside of God. Absolutely
nothing. Let us remember this truth and rely on
God's goodness for every aspect of our lives.

Rather than trying to tackle more than one
can handle or dancing around the truth, it's cru-
cial to ask a simple question when considering
someone – is this person, family, or friend safe?

Have you recently taken the time to sit on the porch with someone, perhaps a relative, both so consumed by weariness and stress that you forgot to look up at the sky, missing the sunset?

Reflect on the tracks and tears of those remaining in the medical field, especially those on the verge of retirement. It's an overwhelming reality. Wave the white flag, kick off your shoes, and try to stand for a moment in their sandals. Don't walk away now; stand side by side, remembering that where two or more are gathered, there is strength. This applies whether it's a couple, a blended family, or any relationship.

On a personal note, thank you, Jesus, for marital bliss in this critical hour. Thank you, Lord God, for reconnecting and uniting families worldwide in ways only you can. Choosing from a selective rack of clothing carries a unique quality. Most of us carefully pick our pieces, while others may rush through the process. Similarly,

Veronica Carter

in life, we've become selective about who we allow into our space, driven by the necessity to protect ourselves. It's important to acknowledge that there will always be silent haters, individuals who make us feel like we don't belong or carry a certain stench that sets us apart. Yet, we thank God for the courage, strength, and will to come just as we are.

Give yourself a round of applause today! It's the recognition of what we don't know that allows us to let go of preconceived ideas and obligations. In this moment, the prevailing thought is, "For with God, nothing shall be impossible."

Reflecting on Romans 9:21-23, we are reminded that the Potter has power over the clay, shaping vessels for honor and dishonor from the same lump. God, in His wisdom, endures with much patience the vessels of wrath prepared for destruction. Simultaneously, He makes known the riches of His glory on the vessels of mercy,

prepared beforehand for glory. It's a powerful re-
minder of God's sovereignty and the intricate
ways He shapes our destinies.

Attention, young people, people in general,
and God's people, before you dive into your con-
trolled devices, take a moment to scroll down
and consider the refreshing blog of the good
news of the Gospel. It's a one-of-a-kind perspec-
tive emanating from the portal and the throne
room of grace, currently centered on the train
amidst God's glorious and ancient angels.

Feel the steady increase in the rumbling,
chugging, hissing, and screeching brakes as the
train slows down, aligning with the surface of
the rails at the next stop. The forlorn sound of
the whistle echoes through the neighborhoods.
Amidst the cacophony of voices talking simulta-
neously, I strain to catch a little bit of informa-
tion.

What I manage to grasp is, "If God is for

you, He is more than the world against you." As I tune in a little closer, I hear something more, something that captivates my attention.

What an incredible God we serve! As I sat there, my fingers twittering away, overwhelming thoughts of gratitude seemed to sweep over me. I started to examine myself, interpreting the many incredible ways to express gratitude. Here's how it sounded:

I could hear multiple voices saying, "If I had a thousand tongues, I could not say thank you enough." It resonates like Whitney Houston, whose homegoing brought us all to church. Then I heard, "Thank you, Lord, for girding up the loins of my mind. Abba! Thank you for awakening the creative genius within me. Thank you, Lord, for revelation knowledge that flows in and through me, giving me the wisdom to articulate it and the God-given knowledge to know when." It sounds like Mister Rogers in his neighborhood, "It's a beautiful day in this neighborhood."

Then I heard, "Thank you, Lord, for when I am reluctant to start something new; you are my bulletproof vest. You are my 'Jehovah Jira,' my provider! You are my 'Elshidi,' the God of more than enough! You are 'Elohim,' powerful and mighty! You are 'Jehovah Raffa,' my healer! My God, I am thine." It captures the essence of gratitude. I could hear all the above. Who is it that you hear? What voice can you relate to? Thank you, Lord, for your intricate, excessive power, reassuring our steps and allowing us to focus not just on what you are doing right now but even more so on what you are about to do.

Thank you, Lord, for being our knowledge bearer when we feel lost. It sounds like Bob Ross, creating beautiful landscapes on the canvas of our lives. Thank you, Lord, for increasing our intellectual capacity, giving us the ability to think and build higher, expanding our brain flow from

Veronica Carter

thoughts to action and procedure to process.

Thank you, Lord, for quick thinking, elaborate energy, and efficient response. Thank you for being the confidence that dwells within us and the overlapping sustaining grace that keeps us, reminiscent of Princess Diana.

Then I heard, "Thank you, Lord, you are the breastplate of righteousness, the one in whom I am delighted to latch onto, always hungry for more. It is no doubt that I am in diligent pursuit. As I stretch forth, I am learning to celebrate small victories, pressing forward towards the mark of glory, still in hot pursuit, ready and eager for yet another touch, if only for the fibrous loose threads of your garment."

Understand like so many I have been through too much just to throw in the towel, I have no choice I cannot let go. Fastening the grip its full speed ahead. Wait a minute that's the hour of the locomotive. My God it's not the Barber, not the

Beautician, nor the Stylist but it is my Voice That I hear.

Psalm 16 vs 6 The Boundary lines have fallen for me in pleasant places; surely I have a delightful inheritance. I must believe that! I have to believe that!

Malachi 4 vs 5-6 " See, I will send the prophet Elijah to you before that great and dreadful day the Lord comes. He will turn the hearts of the parents to their children, and the hearts of the children to their parents; or else I will come and strike the land with total destruction."

If Redemption is in order and Pro-bono was the Staff, then I say Free all of us! We have made mistakes, including Cuomo; everyone knows he did the best he could under uncertainty. That better said if Vote was the option of Choice, it would be nice to go. And for those Leading representatives who have placed their careers secretly on the line to tell us some of these sadistic truths of our History, like 1923. I mean, if I were to speak allegedly or in code like the Politicians who seem to be sipping their own Kool-Aid, while regurgitating the environment of the cult. That's the true spill; no need for a Consultant; I have seen much of what I need to see.

Isaiah 40 vs. 28 Have you not known? Have you not heard? The everlasting God, the Lord, The Creator of the ends of the earth, Neither faints nor is weary. His understanding is unsearchable. He gives power to the weak, And to those who have no might, He increases strength. Never mind who's at fault is, lift up, Stretch-out, and shake it off; embrace the possibility of the Final Analysis. Can you see yourself as God sees you?

2 Chronicles 7:13-16 is a powerful reminder: "If My people who are called by My name will humble themselves, and pray, seek My face, and turn from their wicked ways, then I will hear

from heaven, and will forgive their sin and heal their land."

Closing with the affirmation that "I am a Friend of God" echoes the sentiment from James 2:23, which states, "And the Scripture was fulfilled that says, 'Abraham believed God, and it was credited to him as righteousness,' and he was called God's friend."

May these verses inspire humility, prayer, seeking God's face, and turning from any wicked ways, knowing that through belief and righteousness, we too can be called friends of God.